by Iain Gray

Lang**Syne**

PUBLISHING

WRITING *to* REMEMBER

Lang Syne

PUBLISHING

WRITING *to* REMEMBER

79 Main Street, Newtongrange,
Midlothian EH22 4NA
Tel: 0131 344 0414   Fax: 0845 075 6085
E-mail: info@lang-syne.co.uk
www.langsyneshop.co.uk

Design by Dorothy Meikle
Printed by Printwell Ltd

ISBN 978-1-85217-482-8

Bennett

MOTTO:

To serve the king with right good will.

CREST:

A double scaling ladder as used in sieges.

NAME variations include:
Benet
Benett
Bennet

Chapter one:

The origins of popular surnames

by George Forbes and Iain Gray

**If you don't know where you came from, you won't
know where you're going is a frequently quoted
observation and one that has a particular resonance
today when there has been a marked upsurge in
interest in genealogy, with increasing numbers of
people curious to trace their family roots.**

Main sources for genealogical research
include census returns and official records of births,
marriages and deaths – and the key to unlocking the
detail they contain is obviously a family surname, one
that has been 'inherited' and passed from generation
to generation.

No matter our station in life, we all have a
surname – but it was not until about the middle of the
fourteenth century that the practice of being identified
by a particular surname became commonly established
throughout the British Isles.

Previous to this, it was normal for a person to be identified through the use of only a forename.

But as population gradually increased and there were many more people with the same forename, surnames were adopted to distinguish one person, or community, from another.

Many common English surnames are patronymic in origin, meaning they stem from the forename of one's father – with 'Johnson,' for example, indicating 'son of John.'

It was the Normans, in the wake of their eleventh century conquest of Anglo-Saxon England, a pivotal moment in the nation's history, who first brought surnames into usage – although it was a gradual process.

For the Normans, these were names initially based on the title of their estates, local villages and chateaux in France to distinguish and identify these landholdings.

Such grand descriptions also helped enhance the prestige of these warlords and generally glorify their lofty positions high above the humble serfs slaving away below in the pecking order who had only single names, often with Biblical connotations as in Pierre and Jacques.

The only descriptive distinctions among the peasantry concerned their occupations, like 'Pierre the swineherd' or 'Jacques the ferryman.'

Roots of surnames that came into usage in England not only included Norman-French, but also Old French, Old Norse, Old English, Middle English, German, Latin, Greek, Hebrew and the Gaelic languages of the Celts.

The Normans themselves were originally Vikings, or 'Northmen', who raided, colonised and eventually settled down around the French coastline.

The had sailed up the Seine in their longboats in 900AD under their ferocious leader Rollo and ruled the roost in north eastern France before sailing over to conquer England in 1066 under Duke William of Normandy – better known to posterity as William the Conqueror, or King William I of England.

Granted lands in the newly-conquered England, some of their descendants later acquired territories in Wales, Scotland and Ireland – taking not only their own surnames, but also the practice of adopting a surname, with them.

But it was in England where Norman rule and custom first impacted, particularly in relation to the adoption of surnames.

This is reflected in the famous *Domesday Book*, a massive survey of much of England and Wales, ordered by William I, to determine who owned what, what it was worth and therefore how much they were liable to pay in taxes to the voracious Royal Exchequer.

Completed in 1086 and now held in the National Archives in Kew, London, 'Domesday' was an Old English word meaning 'Day of Judgement.'

This was because, in the words of one contemporary chronicler, "its decisions, like those of the Last Judgement, are unalterable."

It had been a requirement of all those English landholders – from the richest to the poorest – that they identify themselves for the purposes of the survey and for future reference by means of a surname.

This is why the *Domesday Book*, although written in Latin as was the practice for several centuries with both civic and ecclesiastical records, is an invaluable source for the early appearance of a wide range of English surnames.

Several of these names were coined in connection with occupations.

These include Baker and Smith, while Cooks, Chamberlains, Constables and Porters were to be found carrying out duties in large medieval households.

The church's influence can be found in names such as Bishop, Friar and Monk while the popular name of Bennett derives from the late fifth to mid-sixth century Saint Benedict, founder of the Benedictine order of monks.

The early medical profession is represented by Barber, while businessmen produced names that include Merchant and Sellers.

Down at the village watermill, the names that cropped up included Millar/Miller, Walker and Fuller, while other self-explanatory trades included Cooper, Tailor, Mason and Wright.

Even the scenery was utilised as in Moor, Hill, Wood and Forrest – while the hunt and the chase supplied names that include Hunter, Falconer, Fowler and Fox.

Colours are also a source of popular surnames, as in Black, Brown, Gray/Grey, Green and White, and would have denoted the colour of the clothing the person habitually wore or, apart from the obvious exception of 'Green', one's hair colouring or even complexion.

The surname Red developed into Reid, while

Blue was rare and no-one wanted to be associated with yellow.

Rather self-important individuals took surnames that include Goodman and Wiseman, while physical attributes crept into surnames such as Small and Little.

Many families proudly boast the heraldic device known as a Coat of Arms, as featured on our front cover.

The central motif of the Coat of Arms would originally have been what was borne on the shield of a warrior to distinguish himself from others on the battlefield.

Not featured on the Coat of Arms, but high-lighted on page three, is the family motto and related crest – with the latter frequently different from the central motif.

Adding further variety to the rich cultural heritage that is represented by surnames is the appearance in recent times in lists of the 100 most common names found in England of ones that include Khan, Patel and Singh – names that have proud roots in the vast sub-continent of India.

Echoes of a far distant past can still be found in our surnames and they can be borne with pride in commemoration of our forebears.

Chapter two:

Religion and conquest

A surname derived from the given name of Benedict, in turn derived from the Latin 'benedictus', meaning 'blessed', 'Bennett' first became popular throughout the British Isles in the eleventh century in the forms of the Norman-French 'Beneit' and 'Benoit.'

The popularity of Benedict as a given name, particularly during the medieval period, was due to the highly revered Saint Benedict, also known as Benedict of Nursia – now Norcia in the Italian region of Umbria.

Born in about 480 AD, the son of a Roman noble, this Christian saint is recognised as the founder of Western Monasticism.

Founding a religious community at Monte Cassino, in the mountains of southern Italy, he drew up the Rule of Saint Benedict, containing precepts for those who chose to lead a monastic life.

This eventually gave rise to the religious order of the Benedictines, while his precepts also proved popular among other religious orders.

Noted for being 'gentle and disciplined', he died at Monte Cassino in 543 and was canonised by Pope Honorius II in 1220.

Recognised as the patron saint of Europe and of students and also revered by the Lutheran, Eastern Orthodox and Anglican faiths, his Feast Day in the Roman Catholic Calendar of Saints is July 11.

It was for monks from the Order of Savigny, in northern France, and who followed the Rule of Saint Benedict, that Furness Abbey in northern England was originally built.

Founded in 1123 by Stephen, Count of Boulogne, and located in the colourfully named Valley of the Deadly Nightshade between Dalton-in-Furness and Barrow-in-Furness, in the Cumbria region, it later passed to the Cistercian religious order.

Destroyed on the orders of Henry VIII in 1537 during the English Reformation, its silent ruins dominate the local landscape to this day.

It was the Normans, following their conquest of Anglo-Saxon England in 1066, who popularised the given name Benedict – that later also developed into the surname of Bennett.

It was in northern England, in the modern

day county of Durham that early bearers of the Bennett name were to be found.

By 1066, England had become a nation with several powerful competitors to the throne.

In what were extremely complex family, political and military machinations, the monarch was Harold II, who had succeeded to the throne following the death of Edward the Confessor.

But his right to the throne was contested by two powerful competitors – his brother-in-law King Harold Hardrada of Norway, in alliance with Tostig, Harold II's brother, and Duke William II of Normandy.

In what has become known as The Year of Three Battles, Hardrada invaded England and gained victory over the English king on September 20th at the battle of Fulford, in Yorkshire.

Five days later, however, Harold II decisively defeated his brother-in-law and brother at the battle of Stamford Bridge.

But Harold had little time to celebrate his victory, having to immediately march south from Yorkshire to encounter a mighty invasion force, led by Duke William of Normandy that had landed at Hastings, in East Sussex.

Harold's battle-hardened but exhausted force

of Anglo-Saxon soldiers confronted the Normans on October 25th in a battle subsequently depicted on the Bayeux tapestry – a 23ft. long strip of embroidered linen thought to have been commissioned eleven years after the event by the Norman Odo of Bayeux.

It was at the top of Senlac Hill that Harold drew up a strong defensive position, building a shield wall to repel Duke William's cavalry and infantry.

The Normans suffered heavy losses, but through a combination of the deadly skill of their archers and the ferocious determination of their cavalry they eventually won the day.

Anglo-Saxon morale collapsed on the battle-field as word spread through the ranks that Harold had been killed – the Bayeux Tapestry depicting this as having happened when the English king was struck by an arrow to the head.

Amidst the carnage of the battlefield, it was difficult to identify Harold – the last of the Anglo-Saxon kings.

Some sources assert William ordered his body to be thrown into the sea, while others state it was secretly buried at Waltham Abbey.

What is known with certainty, however, is that William in celebration of his great victory, founded Battle Abbey, near the site of the battle, ordering that the altar be sited on the spot where Harold was believed to have fallen.

William was declared King of England on December 25, and what followed was the complete subjugation of his Anglo-Saxon subjects.

Those Normans who had fought on his behalf were rewarded with the lands of Anglo-Saxons, many of whom sought exile abroad as mercenaries.

Within an astonishingly short space of time Norman manners, customs, law and even architecture such as that of Furness Abbey were imposed on England – laying the basis for what subsequently became established 'English' custom and practice.

An early record of the Bennett name appears in the Charter Roll of Durham in 1208, with reference to a William Benet, while a Joanna Benet is recorded in Yorkshire in 1379.

Bearers of the name figure prominently in the historical record.

Born in 1809, Lieutenant Henry Bennett has the dubious distinction of having been the first military officer to die in the service of Queen Victoria in what was the last armed insurrection on English soil.

This was in May of 1838 at the battle of

Bossenden Wood, nearly four miles northwest of Canterbury.

The insurrection was led by the self-proclaimed messiah John Nichols Thom, also known as Mad Tom.

The eccentric Thom, who called himself King of Jerusalem, gathered a large following in Canterbury as he campaigned against the tax law of the day and the Poor Law Amendment Act of 1834.

This ordered that all able-bodied workers, particularly farmers, who could not find work be sent to the humiliating drudgery of the workhouse.

Matters came to a head when Thom, after having promised his deluded followers that they would be able to take over the estates of the landed gentry, confronted the authorities in the form of the military at Bossenden Wood.

Lieutenant Bennett, of the 45th Regiment of Foot (Sherwood Foresters) and in charge of 100 troops, was shot and killed by Thom – while Thom was also shot and killed along with nine of his followers.

Thom was buried in an unmarked grave, while Bennett was buried with full military honours in Canterbury Cathedral in the presence of an estimated 6,000 spectators.

Chapter three:

Heroes and eccentrics

In later centuries and on much different fields of battle, bearers of the Bennett name have also stamped their mark on the historical record.

Born in 1887 in Balwyn, Melbourne, Henry Gordon Bennett, more commonly known as Gordon Bennett, was the Australian Army Lieutenant General who served throughout both the First World War and the Second World War.

Despite serving with heroic distinction throughout the Gallipoli campaign and on the Western Front during the first conflict, he is nevertheless controversially remembered for his actions in the aftermath of the fall of Singapore to the Japanese in March of 1942.

As commander of the Australian 8th Division and subordinate to Lieutenant General Arthur Percival, the British officer commanding Malaya, Bennett was criticised after the Second World War for having disobeyed an order from Percival to surrender to the victorious Japanese.

Bennett, along with a small group of his men,

managed to evade the clutches of the Japanese and make it back to Australia.

The Australian commander was accused after the war of having relinquished his command without permission – while an Australian Royal Commission concluded that he had indeed disobeyed Percival's order.

But the vast majority of the soldiers he had commanded and who had been led into the hell of captivity nevertheless remained fiercely loyal to him.

The recipient of battle honours that include the Distinguished Service Order (DSO), he died in 1962.

Also of Australian birth and a highly decorated officer of the Second World War, Donald Bennett was the pioneering aviator and bomber pilot who commanded the RAF's Pathfinder Force.

Born in 1910 in Toowoomba, Queensland, he joined the Royal Australian Air Force in 1930, transferring to the RAF a year later.

Renowned for his technical and navigational skills, he was described as "one of the most brilliant technical airmen of his generation – an outstanding pilot, a superb navigator who was also capable of stripping a wireless set or overhauling an engine."

Leaving the RAF in 1935 to join Imperial Airways, he specialised in long distance flights and pioneered the complex technique of air-to-air refuelling.

Rejoining the RAF on the outbreak of the Second World War in 1939, he established the Atlantic Ferry Organisation – that delivered American and Canadian-made aircraft to Britain.

Transferred to RAF Coastal Command in April of 1942, Bennett was placed in command of 10 Squadron (Handley-Page Halifax) and led a raid on the German battleship *Tirpitz*.

Shot down during the raid, he and his co-pilot managed to escape to Sweden and later return to Britain.

It was for this that both men were awarded the DSO.

Only a few weeks after his return to Britain, Bennett was placed in command of the Pathfinder Force – that led the bomber streams to the target areas of enemy territory and dropped 'markers' for the bombers to aim at.

By 1943 he had been promoted to Air-Vice Marshall, becoming the youngest person in the RAF to hold such a position.

He died in 1986, having held positions after the war that included director of British South American Airways and also having written his autobiography, *Pathfinder*.

Away from the field of battle, James Gordon Bennett, Sr., made his mark on the historical record as a pioneering figure in American newspapers.

Born in Scotland in 1795 in Newmill, Banffshire, he studied for a time at a Roman Catholic seminary in Aberdeen before immigrating at the age of 24 to North America.

Working for a short period in Halifax, Nova Scotia, as a schoolmaster, he later moved to Portland, Maine, before moving yet again in 1820 to Boston.

Abandoning his career as a teacher, he worked as a bookseller and a proof reader.

By 1823, Bennett was to be found in New York City, working as a freelance newspaper journalist and then as an assistant editor of the *New York Courier and Enquirer*.

Having carefully accumulated his earnings, by 1835 he was able to found and launch the *New York Herald*.

It proved an immediate success, with Bennett giving space for in-depth interviews with victims of crime, witnesses and also leading political figures of the day.

It was the *New York Herald* that had the first 'exclusive' interview with a U.S. President – an interview conducted by Bennett himself in 1839 with President Martin Van Buren.

He died in 1872, having six years earlier passed control of the *New York Herald* to his son, James Gordon Bennett, Jr., and with the newspaper boasting the highest circulation in America.

Born in New York City in 1841, and more commonly known as Gordon Bennett, it was this highly colourful character who gave rise to the well-known expletive *Gordon Bennett!* as an expression of incredulity.

This was through his eccentric behaviour, widely reported in the gossip columns of rival newspapers of the day.

This behaviour infamously included an incident in 1877 when he arrived at the New York mansion of the wealthy May family to celebrate his engagement to the socialite Caroline May.

Bennett arrived late, drunk and belligerent and scandalised the May family and their guests, who represented the cream of New York society, by urinating into a fireplace. The engagement, unsurprisingly, was immediately called off.

When not scandalising society, Bennett found time to further boost the popularity of the newspaper founded by his more soberly behaved father.

It was the *New York Herald*, for example, that under his proprietorship funded Henry Morton Stanley's expedition to Africa in 1869 to find the Scots missionary and explorer Dr David Livingstone.

Stanley was successful in his quest, and the newspaper obtained the exclusive story of his adventures and encounter with Livingstone.

It was also one of the first instances of when a newspaper earned a substantial sum of money by later syndicating the story on a world-wide basis to other newspapers.

Indulging his flamboyant tastes to the full, Bennett pursued passions that included yachting.

Commodore of the New York Yacht Club, in 1866 he won the first trans-oceanic yacht race, while he also founded the Westchester Polo Club – America's first such club.

Taking to the skies, it was in 1906 that he established the Gordon Bennett Cup in ballooning – a cup that is competed for to this day.

Later settling in Paris, he launched the *Paris Herald*, a French edition of the *New York Herald*, and the forerunner of today's *International Herald Tribune*.

He died in 1918 and the newspaper founded by his father was later merged with its rival, the *New York Tribune*.

Asteroid 305 Gordonia is named in his honour.

From the flamboyancy of Gordon Bennett to the rather more serious realm of politics, Richard Bedford Bennett, better known as R.B. Bennett, served from August of 1930 to October of 1935 as 11th Prime Minister of Canada.

Born in 1870 at Hopewell Hill, New Brunswick, the descendant of a family who had immigrated to North America from England in the seventeenth century, he became friendly as a youth with Max Aitken – the future press baron better known as Lord Beaverbrook.

It was during his time in his native Canada that Beaverbrook helped to further the political career of Bennett.

Becoming the first leader of the Alberta Conservative Party in 1905, Bennett was elected six years later to the Canadian House of Commons.

In 1930, by which time he was leader of the overall Canadian Conservative Party, he took office as 11th Prime Minister of Canada.

This was at the time of the world-wide economic depression and great fear in democratic nations such as Canada of Communist subversion.

It was in reaction to this fear that Bennett controversially invoked a special code of the Criminal Code of Canada that allowed harsh penalties against any individual or organisation, including trades unions, deemed as a threat to the established order.

So harsh was this code that he became known as "Iron Heel Bennett."

Leaving active politics in 1938 he settled in England, where six years before his death in 1947 he was elevated to the Peerage of the United Kingdom as Viscount Bennett – the first and only former Canadian Prime Minister to be so honoured.

Chapter four:

On the world stage

Born in 1926 in Queens, New York City, Anthony Dominick Benedetto is the American singer of popular music, show tunes and jazz better known as Tony Bennett.

The son of an Italian immigrant grocer and a seamstress, it was not until after serving as an infantryman during the Second World War that he took up singing as a career.

He had his first hit single in 1951 with *Because of You*, followed by a string of others that include his 1962 'signature' song *I Left My Heart in San Francisco* – which won him a Grammy Award for Best Solo Vocal Performance.

Now the recipient of no fewer than sixteen other Grammy Awards, including a Lifetime Achievement Award, he is also a highly accomplished artist, painting under his birth name of Anthony Benedetto.

Joining Cliff Richard and The Shadows in 1961 as a replacement for Tony Meehan, **Brian Bennett** is the drummer, composer, arranger and record producer born in 1940 in Palmers Green, North London.

Since leaving The Shadows, he has forged a successful career as the composer of a number of popular television theme tunes that include the themes for BBC's *Rugby Special*, BBC *Golf*, *Birds of a Feather*, *New Tricks* and *The Ruth Rendell Mysteries*.

Inducted into the Rock and Roll Hall of Fame two years before her death in 2009, **Estelle Bennett,** born in 1941, was one of the members of the 1960s' American all-female band The Ronettes.

Born in 1952 in St. Elizabeth, Jamaica, **Lorna Bennett** is the reggae singer best known for her 1972 hit *Breakfast in Bed* – a reggae version of a Dusty Springfield song

Born in Brooklyn, New York City, in 1918, **Roy C. Bennett** is the famed American songwriter who, along with Sid Tepper, wrote a number of hits for Elvis Presley and much of the music for his films, including *Blue Hawaii*.

The duo also wrote for other stars, including Tony Bennett and Rosemary Clooney.

The recipient of numerous awards, **Sir Richard Bennett**, born in 1936 in Broadstairs, Kent, is the English composer of film scores that include those for the 1967 *Far from the Madding Crowd* and the 1974 *Murder on the Orient Express*.

On the stage, one noted American acting dynasty was one founded by **Richard Bennett**, born in 1870 in Deacon Mills, Indiana.

A star mainly of the silent era of film, he is also remembered for his role in the 1942 *The Magnificent Ambersons*.

Before his death in 1944, he once famously described the movie industry as "not a business, but a madhouse."

Married to the actress Adrienne Morrison, he was the father of successful actresses.

Born in 1904 in New York City, his daughter **Constance Bennett** was a star of films that include the 1922 *What's Wrong with the Women?*, the 1929 *This Thing Called Love* and, from 1937, *Topper*.

The recipient of a star on the Hollywood Walk of Fame, she died in 1965.

She was the sister of **Joan Bennett**, also the recipient of a star on the Hollywood Walk of Fame, and noted for her roles in films that include director Fritz Lang's 1944 *The Woman in the Window* and his 1945 *Scarlet Street*.

Born in 1910, she died in 1990.

In contemporary acting, **Hywel Bennett**, born in 1944 in Carmarthenshire, Wales is the television actor best known for his role in the 1979-1984 British television sitcom *Shelley* and as Ricky Tarr in the acclaimed 1979 television adaptation of John le Carre's spy thriller *Tinker Tailor Soldier Spy*.

The recipient of a Canadian Gemini Award for Best Supporting Actor in a Drama Series for his role as the vampire Lucien LeCroix in the *Forever Knight* television series, **Nigel Bennett** is the English actor, writer and director born in 1949 in Wolverhampton.

Resident in Canada since the mid-1980s, his big screen credits include the 2000 *The Crossing*.

Born in 1928 in Beckenham, Kent, **John Bennett** was the English actor whose many British television credits include *The Avengers*, *Bergerac*, *The Saint* and the sitcom *Porridge*; he died in 2005.

Married to the playwright John Osborne, **Jill Bennett** was the actress of stage and screen whose film credits include the 1965 *The Nanny*, in which she starred beside Bette Davis, and the 1990 *The Sheltering Sky*.

Born to British parents in 1931 in Penang, Straits Settlements, she died in 1990.

Born in 1934 in Armley, Leeds, **Alan Bennett** is the award-winning English playwright, screenwriter and actor who first rose to fame through his collaboration with Peter Cook, Dudley Moore and Jonathan Miller in the revue *Beyond the Fringe* at the 1960 Edinburgh Film Festival.

Abandoning his career as a teacher of medieval history in favour of full-time writing, he has become noted for his series of television monologues in addition to screenwriting films that include the 1991 *The Madness of King George*.

The recipient of awards that include the Laurence Olivier Award for Outstanding Contribution to British Theatre, he has declined the honours of a CBE and a knighthood – saying it would be akin to having to wear a suit for the rest of his life.

Born in 1899 in Shoreham-by-Sea, Sussex, **Charles Bennett** was the English playwright and screenwriter responsible for a number of director Alfred Hitchcock films that include the 1934 *The Man Who Knew Too Much*, the 1935 *The 39 Steps* and, from 1940, *Foreign Correspondent*. He died in 1955.

Not only a novelist but also a journalist and government propagandist, **Arnold Bennett** was born in 1867 in Hanley, Staffordshire.

A regular contributor to the *London Evening Standard*, he also served during the First World War at the Ministry of Information as director of propaganda for France.

As a novelist, he is best known for works that include his 1898 *A Man from the North*, the *Clayhanger* trilogy and *Riceyman Steps*, winner of the 1923 James Tait Black Memorial Prize; he died in 1931.

Bearers of the Bennett name have also excelled, and continue to excel, in the highly competitive world of sport.

In basketball, **Tony Bennett**, born in 1969 in Green Bay, Wisconsin, was a member of the U.S. team that won the bronze medal at the 1991 Pan American Games.

Born in 1924 in Heavener, Oklahoma, **A.L. Bennett** was a member of the Oklahoma State University's 1945-1946 National Championship team; he died in 2008.

From basketball to the swimming pool, **Brooke Bennett** is the female triple-Olympic champion born in 1980 in Plant City, Florida.

She won the gold medal in the 800-metres freestyle event at the 1996 Olympics, and gold in both the 400-metres freestyle and 800-metres freestyle in 2000.

From swimming to SCUBA diving, **John Bennett**, born in 1959, was the British diver who, in November of 2001, became the first person to 'deep dive' below a depth of 1,000-feet using self-controlled breathing apparatus.

He disappeared during a diving incident in Korea in March of 2004, and declared legally dead two years later; his body has never been recovered.

From sport to art, Charles Henry Bennett, better known as **Charles H. Bennett**, was a Victorian pioneer of comic illustration.

Born in London in 1828, he illustrated a number of children's books, most notably a version of *Aesop's Fables*. His work also appeared in a number of newspapers and comic publications such as *Punch* magazine.

Despite his artistic genius and high demand for his work, he died in poverty at the age of 37.

In contemporary times, **Clay Bennett** is the American newspaper cartoonist born in 1958 in Clinton, South Carolina.

Winner of the 2002 Pulitzer Prize for *Editorial Cartooning* and recipient of the 2011 United

Nations Political Cartoon Award, his work is syndicated by the Washington Post Writers Group.

One particularly inventive bearer of the Bennett name was the electrical engineer **Alfred Bennett**.

Born in 1850 in Islington, London, he carried out pioneering work in the early 1880s on incandescent electric lighting in addition to inventing ceramic telegraph insulation, a telephone transformer and an iron-alkali battery.

Before his death in 1928, he had also been responsible for helping to establish and maintain telephone systems in such diverse locations that include Guernsey, Portsmouth, Brighton and Glasgow.

Yet another pioneering technologist was the Australian computer scientist **Professor John Makepeace Bennett**.

Born in 1921 in Warwick, Queensland, and carrying out much of his work at the University of Sydney, he was Australia's first professor of computer science and founding president of the Australian Computer Society.

Appointed and Officer of the Order of Australia and the recipient in 2001 of the nation's Centenary Medal for service to computer science and technology, he died in 2010.